Galaxies

ISAAC ASIMOV

IRREGULAR GALAXY IN URSA MAJOR

Paintings by Alex Ebel and Denny McMains

FOLLETT PUBLISHING COMPANY **Chicago   New York**

Library of Congress Catalog Card Number: 68-13034   FIRST PRINTING   TLA 3315

The Mayans built this observatory
in Mexico about 1,000 years ago. They
had no telescopes.

For many thousands of years, men have watched the Sun, the Moon, the planets, and the stars move in the sky.

They wanted to know what these lights in the sky were, and how they got there, and why they moved the way they did.

These astronomers, or sky-watchers, used only their eyes at first. Not much can be seen that way.

In 1608, things changed. A tube with lenses, or curved pieces of glass, was pointed at the sky. The lenses collected light and drew it together into a bright spot. The Moon appeared larger. Mountains could be seen on it. The planets looked like worlds instead of like stars. And stars that were too dim to see with the eyes alone were made visible.

The tube with lenses was the telescope.

In later years, astronomers made better and better telescopes. And about 50 years after the first telescope was built, accurate clocks were built for the first time. Now astronomers could tell exactly how long it took a star or a planet or some other body in space to move a certain distance.

Today's astronomers use atomic clocks. The measurement of time is important in finding star distances and many other things.

A piece of glass called a prism breaks up white light into its many colors, called the spectrum. The dark or bright lines in the spectrum help astronomers know what the star is made of.

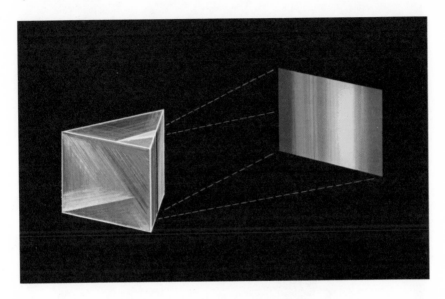

In the 1800's, scientists found how to break up the light from stars into many colors. They used a tool called a spectroscope.

By studying the light with a spectroscope, astronomers could tell whether stars were coming toward us or moving away. They could tell how hot stars were. They could even tell what stars were made of.

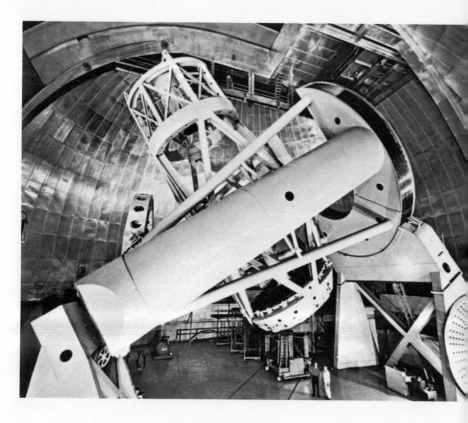

The camera was also invented in the 1800's.
For the first time, pictures could be taken of
the sky. The stars could be studied closely, day
and night.

Most important of all, the camera could take
pictures of stars that were too dim to be seen
by a man looking through a telescope.

The astronomer's workshop is called an observatory. It is built in a place where the air is clean and clear of clouds. Often it is high on a mountain, away from bright lights of the city that blot out starlight.

The roof of an observatory can be opened. The telescope points out through this opening. The whole top of the observatory can turn around so that the opening faces any part of the sky that interests the astronomer.

The observatory holds the most important tools of the astronomer: telescopes, clocks, spectroscopes, cameras, computers, measuring instruments, and a library of photographs and catalogs of objects in the sky.

9

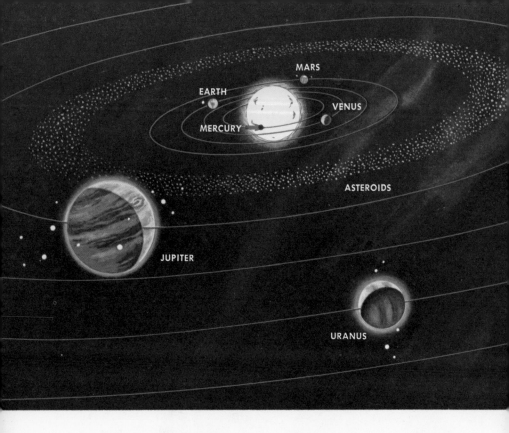

The UNIVERSE is a name given to the Earth, the Sun, the planets, the stars in space, and every other heavenly body that we know about.

At first, astronomers thought that the Earth was the center of the universe. They believed that all heavenly bodies turned about the Earth, as they seemed to do.

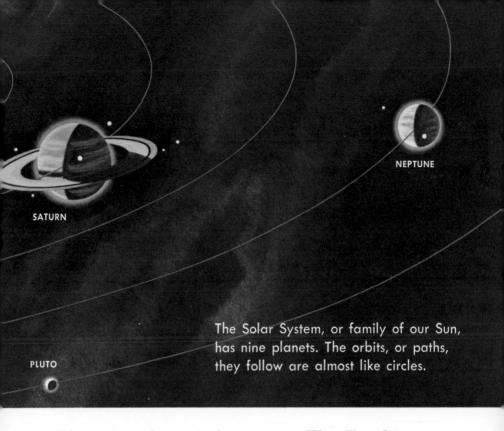

NEPTUNE

SATURN

PLUTO

The Solar System, or family of our Sun, has nine planets. The orbits, or paths, they follow are almost like circles.

This turned out to be wrong. The Earth moves around the Sun, and so do the other planets. The force that keeps the planets moving in their orbits, or paths, is gravity.

Gravity is the pull of each body on every other body. Small bodies pull weakly. But the huge Sun pulls very strongly. It keeps all the planets moving around it.

11

Far out beyond the planets are the stars. Our Sun is a star that happens to be the nearest one to us. That is why we see it as a large, glowing ball in the sky. The other stars are so far away that we see them only as tiny points of light.

Scientists measure the distance between the stars by finding the time it takes for a ray of light to come from the star to Earth. Light travels very quickly — about 186,000 miles in one second. Light comes from the Sun to the Earth in about eight minutes.

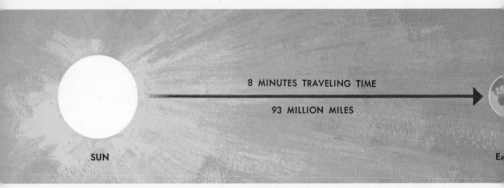

8 MINUTES TRAVELING TIME

93 MILLION MILES

SUN

EA

The Sun is 93 million miles away. Its light reaches us in about 8 minutes. An astronomer would say that the Sun was "8 light-minutes" away from Earth.

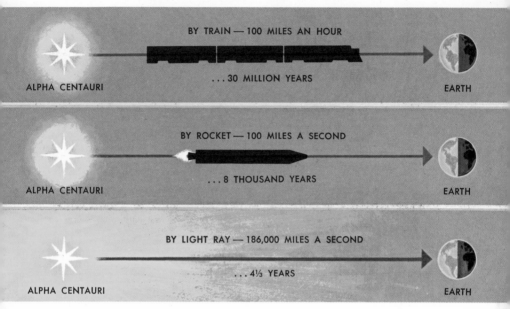

BY TRAIN — 100 MILES AN HOUR

...30 MILLION YEARS

ALPHA CENTAURI · EARTH

BY ROCKET — 100 MILES A SECOND

...8 THOUSAND YEARS

ALPHA CENTAURI · EARTH

BY LIGHT RAY — 186,000 MILES A SECOND

...4⅓ YEARS

ALPHA CENTAURI · EARTH

Light from the nearest star, Alpha Centauri, takes much, much longer to reach Earth. It must travel days, weeks, months, years. Finally, after four years and four months, light from the nearest star would reach Earth.

In one year, light travels about six trillion miles. Astronomers call this distance a LIGHT-YEAR. They say that Alpha Centauri is more than four light-years from our Sun.

13

We can see thousands of stars if we look
up at the night sky. With a telescope, an
astronomer can see many billions. If he takes a
picture through the telescope, still more stars
are shown.

Probably most stars are single, like our
Sun. But some come in pairs, or even in groups
of three or more. There are star clusters made
up of hundreds of stars that are close together
and moving together.

14

Here on Earth, we see the stars in groups called CONSTELLATIONS. The groups seem to stay the same from year to year, and keep the same shapes.

But the stars are not standing still. They are moving through space. They are so far away that it takes many years for their movement to show itself. Our Sun and its family of planets are moving, too.

All of the stars we see seem to be moving rapidly around and around one place in space.

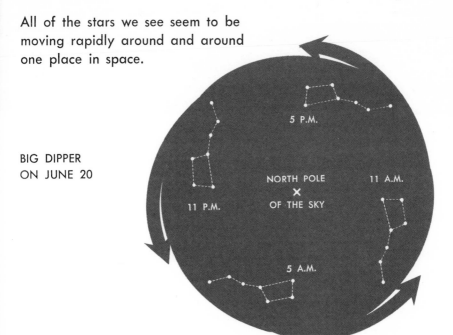

BIG DIPPER
ON JUNE 20

5 P.M.

NORTH POLE
X
OF THE SKY

11 A.M.

11 P.M.

5 A.M.

Our Sun belongs to a huge group
of stars, 100,000 light-years across.
It looks something like this star group.

Our Sun is part of a great gathering of many billions of stars. This is shaped like a pin-wheel and it turns around and around in space. There is a thick cluster of stars at the center of the pin-wheel, and streams of stars called spiral arms come from the center. Our Sun is out in one of the spiral arms, far from the center.

16

When we look through the pin-wheel of stars long-ways, we can see a band of many faint stars that make a dim, milky glow in the sky. This is called the Milky Way.

The great group of stars we belong to is called a GALAXY. Our own Milky Way Galaxy is just one of the many galaxies in space.

17

The space between the stars is not empty. There are huge clouds of dust and gas there. A cloud in space is called a NEBULA. It is not like a rain cloud on Earth.

When a nebula has stars inside it, it may glow brightly. The Great Nebula in Orion is a beautiful bright nebula.

GREAT NEBULA IN ORION

The Horsehead Nebula in Orion is a dark cloud of gas that is outlined against the bright stars behind it.

Nebulae far from stars do not glow. These dark nebulae hide the stars behind them. There are so many dark nebulae behind the nearer stars of the Milky Way that they hide the stars of the center of our galaxy. We can never see the center of the Milky Way, or the spiral arms opposite us.

GREAT GALAXY IN ANDROMEDA

Elsewhere in space there are galaxies just as huge as our own. In the constellation of Andromeda, we can see a small hazy spot of light. A large telescope shows that this spot is another great galaxy, more than two million light-years away from our Milky Way Galaxy.

Our own galaxy is shaped much like the Andromeda Galaxy.

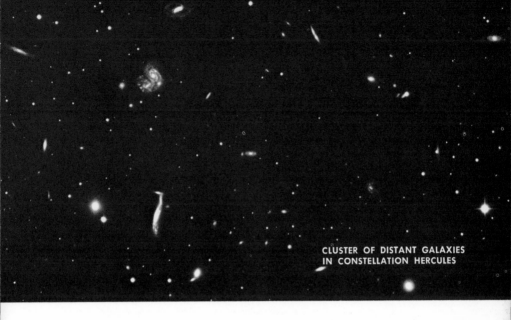

CLUSTER OF DISTANT GALAXIES
IN CONSTELLATION HERCULES

Beyond the Andromeda Galaxy in every direction are still other galaxies. Many of them have pin-wheel shapes and are called spiral galaxies. Other galaxies without spiral arms look like great balls of stars or have no special shape.

All the galaxies put together and the space between them make up the universe. Astronomers do not know how many galaxies there are in the universe. Millions can be seen with large telescopes. There may be many that are farther than we can see.

It is very hard for astronomers to study the galaxies that are very far out in space. Their light is too dim. But radio waves travel as fast as light rays. And in the 1930's, astronomers learned how to study the radio waves given off by the stars and the distant galaxies. Special radio telescopes pick up these radio waves.

The huge radio telescope at Jodrell Bank, England, gathers faint radio waves coming from far parts of the universe.

Our own Milky Way Galaxy is one of a cluster of galaxies. All the clusters of galaxies that are outside our own cluster are moving away from us. The farther away a group of galaxies is, the faster it moves away from us. It seems that the galaxies are speeding away from us because the whole universe is getting bigger, or expanding.

Imagine that galaxies are spots on a balloon. As you blow the balloon up, the spots get farther and farther away from the balloon's center and from each other. A tiny person standing on one spot would see all the other spots speeding away from him. This is what seems to be happening in the universe.

Why are the galaxies moving? Scientists are not sure. Some astronomers think that billions of years ago all the matter in the universe was crowded into one big ball. Then suddenly it exploded. The pieces formed clusters of galaxies and these are still moving farther and farther apart.

This is called the "big bang" theory.

If the "big bang" theory is true, then the universe must have been quite different long ago. Galaxies must have had more dust and gas after they first formed. They must have been hotter and closer together.

Astronomers are trying to study the very edges of the universe. Light coming from there must have started on its way to us billions of years ago. Astronomers hope that this very old light will tell them what things were like when the universe was first formed.

Very recently, astronomers have discovered special kinds of radio waves that seem to have been speeding through space for billions of years. Perhaps these radio waves started out at the time of the "big bang" itself.

Perhaps astronomers are tuning in on the beginning of our universe.

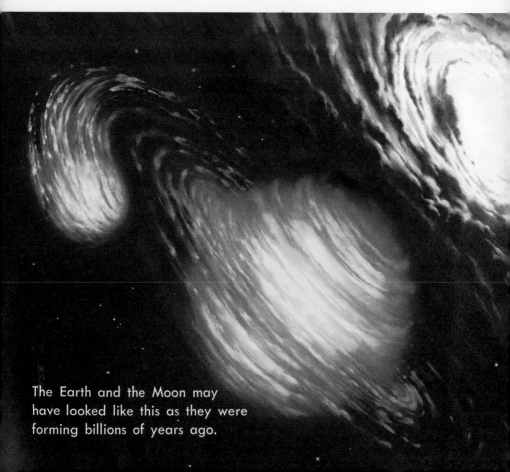

The Earth and the Moon may have looked like this as they were forming billions of years ago.

DUST CLOUDS IN THE CONSTELLATION MONOCEROS

How huge our universe is! There are many billions of stars like our Sun here in our own Milky Way Galaxy. There must be billions more in the other galaxies far out in space.

Most astronomers think that as stars form, dust and gas around them gather into planets. And perhaps some of the Sun-like stars have planets like our Earth.

A planet the size and temperature of our
Earth might be much like the Earth in other
ways. Living things might exist on some
Earth-like planets — perhaps on nearly all of
them. Some of these living things might be as
intelligent as mankind. Some of them might
have better brains than we do and know more
than we do.

The stars in the universe are separated
by huge distances. It will be difficult to cross
the space between one star and another.

But radio waves can cross this space.
Perhaps intelligent beings are sending out
radio signals to reach anyone who might listen
and understand.

Perhaps some day we may discover the
signals of other beings who live on a world
circling another star. Perhaps some day we
will find that we are not alone in the universe.

29

STARS OF THE AUTUMN SKY
OCTOBER 15: 9:00 P.M.

Spiral Galaxy
ANDROMEDA

MILKY

PISCES THE FISHES

CETUS THE WHALE

LAC
THE L

GREAT SQUARE

EAST

Circlet

PEGASUS
THE FLYING HOR

ecliptic

AQUARIUS THE
WATER-BEARER

SOUTH

WORDS YOUNGER CHILDREN MAY NEED HELP WITH

(Numbers refer to the page on which the word first appears.)

4	astronomers	9	observatory	17	galaxy
5	lenses	10	universe	18	nebula
	collected		heavenly	19	opposite
	visible	11	gravity	20	Andromeda
	telescope	13	Alpha Centauri	23	expanding
	scientists	14	thousands	24	exploded
6	accurate		billions		theory
	distance	15	constellations	28	temperature
7	spectroscope	16	spiral		intelligent

THINGS TO DO

Find the Milky Way. The stars of the Milky Way cannot be seen when the bright lights of the city shine upon cloudy, smoky air. But if you are in a place where the sky is clear and there are no lights, you will see a "river" of faint stars stretching across the sky. When you look at a part of the Milky Way, you are looking lengthwise through the great galaxy of which our Sun is a part. Is the Milky Way the same width all across the sky? Why are its individual stars so faint?

The center of our galaxy is in the direction of the constellation Sagittarius. This star group appears in the southern sky during summer. Is the Milky Way brighter in the region of Sagittarius?

Great clouds of dark dust hide many of the stars in our galaxy from the view of astronomers. The dust is thickest in the parts of the sky where the Milky Way gleams. You know that our galaxy is shaped like a wheel. Can you think why most of the dust should be in line with the Milky Way? If you were an astronomer who wanted to look deep into space in order to see distant galaxies, would you search the sky close to the Milky Way? Why not?

Find the Andromeda Galaxy. The photograph on page 20 shows the wheel-shaped Andromeda Galaxy, which is tipped a little. Using this diagram as a guide, try to locate the constellation Andromeda and its galaxy, which is more easily seen with binoculars or a small telescope. Notice the two small satellite galaxies nearby. Our own galaxy has two satellites, too. They are only visible to sky-watchers in the Southern Hemisphere and resemble two faint pieces of the Milky Way or two faintly gleaming clouds. Our satellite galaxies are called the Great and Small Magellanic Clouds. They are irregular in shape and about 200,000 light-years away from our galaxy.

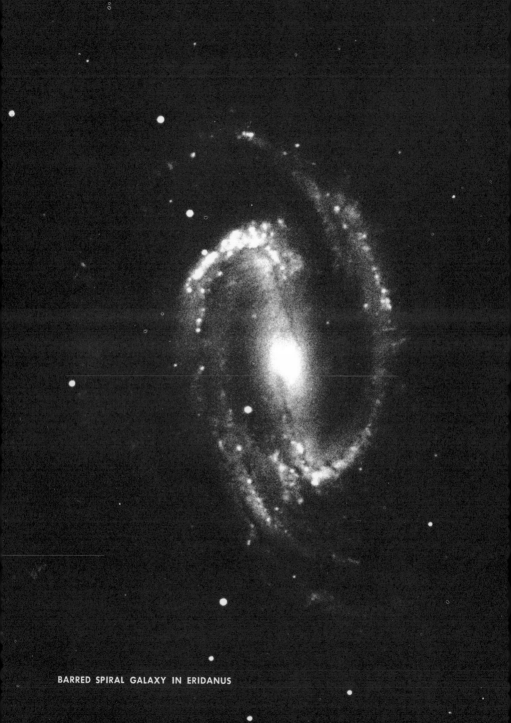

BARRED SPIRAL GALAXY IN ERIDANUS